Off to a Flying Start

Horsing Around the Language

Bill Tivenan and Cassandra Cook
with illustrations by
Ana Mirela Tache

Copyright © 2009 by Bill Tivenan and Cassandra Cook

All rights reserved.

No part of this book may be reproduced or transmitted in any form or by any means, electronic or mechanical, including photocopying, recording, or by any information storage and retrieval system, without permission in writing from the authors. Email inquiries to info@offtoaflyingstartpress.com.

Published by Aardvark Global Publishing Company
Salt Lake City, Utah

www.offtoaflyingstartpress.com

ISBN 978-1-4276-4026-0

Printed in the United States of America

First Printing May 2009

10 9 8 7 6 5 4 3 2 1

For all the horses

Entries

In the Running	44
Inside Track	45
Jockey for Position	46
Long in the Tooth	48
Long Shot	50
Neck and Neck	51
Odds-On	52
Off and Running	53
Off to a Flying Start	54
Off to the Races	56
On One's High Horse	57
On One's Toes	58
On the Money	59
On the Nose	59
One for the Books	60
Out of the Clouds	62
Out of the Gate	63
Photo Finish	64
Put Through One's Paces	66
Put Your Money on the Line	67
Rank Outsider	68
Ride for a Fall	70
Run Circles Around	71
Run True to Form	72
Set the Pace	73
Start from Scratch	74
Straight from the Horse's Mouth	76
Take in Stride	78
Too Close to Call	79
Under the Wire	80

Introduction

The idea for this book came to us last summer, as we were standing in the paddock area at Saratoga Race Course. We'd just seen a horse with his tongue tied off to one side (which we were told they don't mind), and we wondered, "Is that where the term "tongue-tied" comes from?" A few summers before, while on a tour of the barns at a training track in Kentucky, we'd learned that the phrase "get your goat" originated in the world of horse racing. We were so fascinated by this that we'd been repeating it to anyone who would listen ever since. What if we collected popular horse racing expressions in a book to show what an influence the sport has had on everyday language?

From that simple beginning, we started doing research and paying attention to phrasing and clichés that we had used automatically, without ever really thinking about their origins before. For instance, many horse terms that describe the competition of the race have migrated to the world of politics, and we heard them all as we watched the television coverage of the 2008 United States presidential race. A "long shot" candidate and primaries projected as "too close to call" readily come to mind. But so do "down to the wire" and "neck and neck." We were surprised to discover how many phrases got their start at the track. The origins of some entries in this

Introduction

book are not precisely known, but the fact that there is a connection to the equestrian world is always clear. Unfortunately, "tongue-tied" turned out to have nothing to do with horses but rather is a congenital oral defect in humans.

This is no scholarly publication nor is it an exhaustive compendium of all the terms and phrases connected to horses and racing. It is a collection of our favorites and the ones most commonly used even by people who have never seen a horse race or been to the track. Our primary research source was the *Oxford English Dictionary* (Second Edition).

In keeping with the light tone of our subject matter, we wanted this book to reflect our feelings about the game of horse racing. We derive a large amount of pleasure (and sometimes great sadness) from following the races, talking and reading about horses and their personalities, and, of course, placing a wager or two. We hope that both horse racing fans and those interested in the English language will find our work useful and enjoyable.

Bill Tivenan and Cassandra Cook
May 2009

Off to a Flying Start

A Leg Up

Everyone needs a leg up sometimes, but especially jockeys, because of their small size and the imposing size of a racehorse. Before the start of a race, a groom or trainer holds out his hands for the jockey to step into and then the jockey swings onto the horse. Now widely used to describe any act of providing someone with extra help. The phrase sometimes indicates a position of advantage over the competition.

A Head Start

In early horse racing, a horse with "a head start" was given an advantage of up to several lengths over other horses in a race to equalize the competition. In everyday speech, the phrase is now often modified to "getting a head start" and implies any early preparation or beginning that gives someone an edge or an advantage.

"The best students always get a head start on studying for their final exams."

A Horse of a Different Color

First used in horse racing when one placed a bet on a horse of a certain color or on the color of the jockey's silks only to see another horse win the race. The colorful silks a jockey wears represent the owner of the horse. Often stated when a plan is changed or the topic of a debate shifts from what was originally being considered.

"Winning the primary is one thing, but whether she can win the general election is a horse of a different color."

A Real Horse Race

When used to describe a race, the operative word "real" conjures images of *neck-and-neck* battles and *photo finishes*. As most racing fans know, races between horses are not always close or particularly hard fought, and thus there is a need to distinguish a particularly exciting or "real horse race." Outside the racing world, the expression refers to any closely fought contest or competition.

> *"With finalists as talented as these, we can expect a real horse race for the prize."*

A Run for One's Money

Horse racing fans often bet the horses they like rather than the ones that are favored to win. It's true that the odds are longer and they will have bigger winnings if their pick comes in first, but when the horse and jockey gives it their all they don't always mind if they lose. Some of our greatest pleasures in racing have come from watching a losing horse run a close race. We lose a few bucks, but we get plenty of value along the way. These are the circumstances that bettors are describing when they say that the horse gave them a run for their money. In everyday speech, this phrase is used to signify any good competition whether betting is involved or not.

"The child prodigy gave the lead violinist a run for his money."

No sport is pure, and this idiom comes from a race where jockeys would hold back their own mounts and chase or "shoo in" the winner. Races were most assuredly fixed in this way when a group of jockeys had gotten together to bet on the outcome. A shoo-in now means a predetermined and certain winner.

A Shoo-In

Across the Board

If you are betting across the board, your horse must win, place, or show if you are to collect on the bet. The board referred to here is the tote board that shows odds and payouts for a race. The phrase now broadly means to cover all categories without exception. You will often hear it associated with contracts and negotiations.

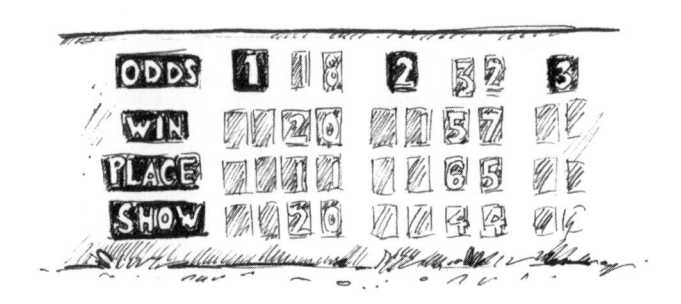

"The wage increases will be implemented across the board."

Also-Ran

A horse in a race who does not finish first, second, or third. On official lists of the order of finish, any horse that is not among the top three finishers is labeled an "also-ran." The term is used to describe any unsuccessful participant in a contest. Outside of racing, its meaning has evolved to contain the implication that the loser is someone or something of inferior qualities.

"Just one scandal is all it takes to turn a leading candidate into an also-ran."

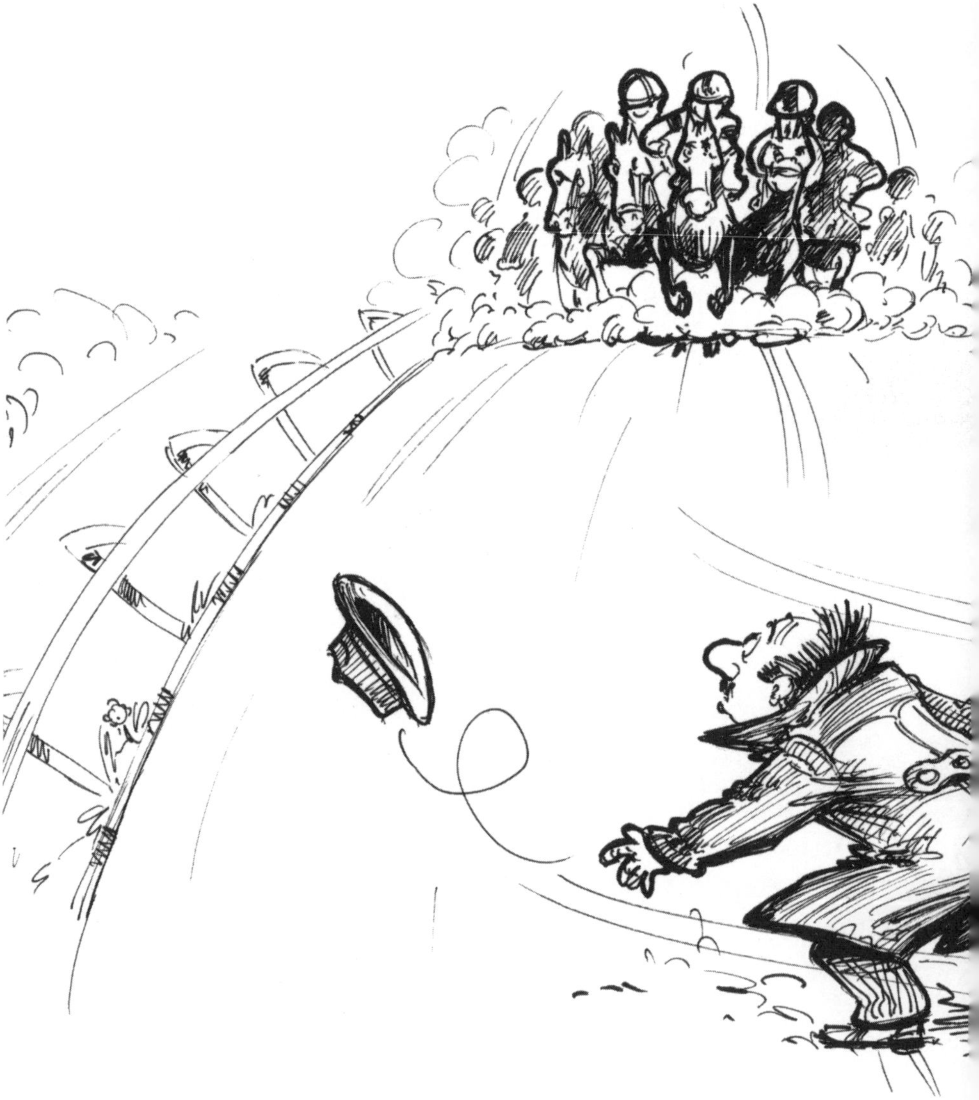

At the Drop of a Hat

In the early years of horse racing in the United States, the start of a race was sometimes signaled by dropping a hat or making a sweeping downward motion with a hat in hand. Ironically, the phrase is now frequently used to describe when something happens at a moment's notice and without any prompting.

Back the Wrong Horse

Anyone who bets money on a horse that does not win has backed the wrong horse. Now widely used to signify a misjudgment concerning the outcome of political contests or other power struggles. It also means to give support to a losing side in a competition, and can also imply the loss of an advantageous position.

"She discovered she had backed the wrong horse when the company she invested in filed for bankruptcy."

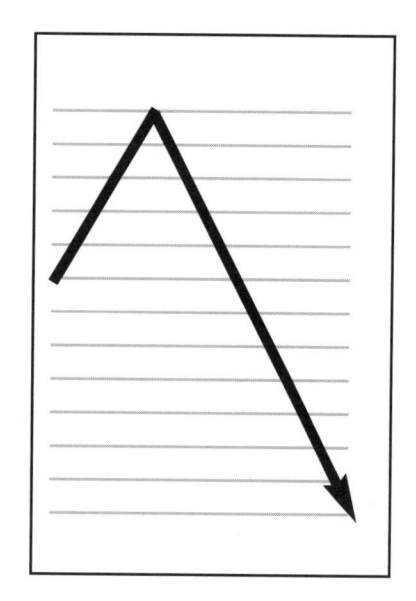

Beat a Dead Horse

We've watched jockeys forcefully apply the whip to a horse even though they are clearly at the limits of their energy and are hopelessly out of contention in a race. This is the kind of misguided and futile effort that "beating a dead horse" describes. In common language, the term refers to a refusal to give up on something even when there is nothing useful left to be done or said.

"We've been through this already. There's no sense beating a dead horse!"

Break Away from the Pack

It's a thrill when one horse surges forward until it is alone in front of the field. As exciting as "breaking away from the pack" is, it does not always lead to a win. There are many horses that get a large lead but cannot sustain it in the later stages of a race. In general the phrase describes an individual who severs connections with a group.

By a Nose

In horse racing the degree of victory is indicated by how far in front the horses have finished. This is measured in lengths, a neck, a head, or a nose. Though not a precise measurement, a win "by a nose" is the slimmest margin of victory. The term is now used to describe beating an opponent by the narrowest amount possible.

A skate is a slang term for an old or run-down horse. A "cheapskate" now commonly refers to a stingy, miserly person, someone who tries to get something for nothing or tries to avoid paying their fair share.

Cheapskate

Chomping at the Bit

Horses are guided as their riders alternately pull back and ease up on the reins attached to a metal piece—or "bit"—in the horse's mouth. A horse that is "chomping" is biting impatiently at the bit, trying to run faster even while being held back by his rider. The related phrase "take the bit in one's teeth" describes a horse who has defied his jockey, taken firm hold of the bit, and begun to run full out. Though top speed is seemingly desirable in a horse race, it is often better for horses to conserve their energy earlier in a race and save it for an all-out run at the end. Used more broadly to describe someone who is eager to get going or impatient at being delayed, or who has taken power in a situation by wresting control from another.

Cinch

The term refers to the strap that holds a saddle firmly in place on a horse. It is now commonly used to describe something that is a sure thing, easily accomplished or mastered.

"It's a cinch we'll get this done in time."

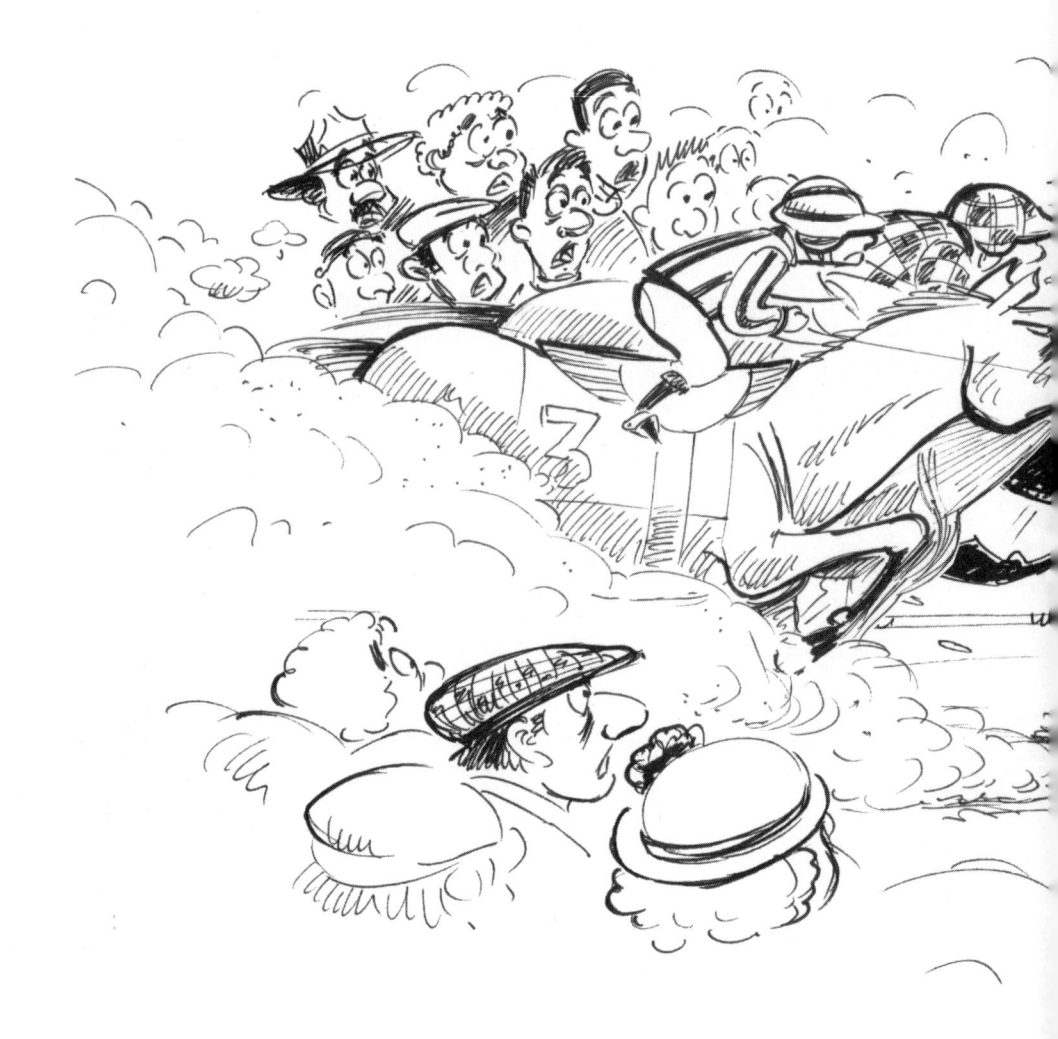
3

Dark Horse

This expression originally referred to a horse that came into a race without an established track record but then unexpectedly won over better-known foes. It is now often applied within the political context, usually to describe a candidate who seems to come from out of nowhere to surprisingly win an election.

Dead Heat

A race in which two or more horses cross the finish line at the same time. The designation of "dead heat" or DH is part of the official lexicon for recording the finishing order of a race. The term is commonly applied to situations where two or more competitors are equally matched and have finished a contest in a tie. In political races the expression is often used to describe an election decided by just a few votes or, in racing language, by a nose.

Dead Ringer

Slang for a horse that has been fraudulently substituted for another in a race. Dead in this phrase means precise or exact as in "dead center" or "dead-on." Today it is much harder to substitute one horse for another since all racehorses now have a unique tattoo on the inside of their upper lip which is checked before a race. Now commonly used to describe any type of a look-alike or duplicate. Dead ringer is one of the more colorful phrases that originated in the world of horse racing. It conjures up images of scam artists and grifters.

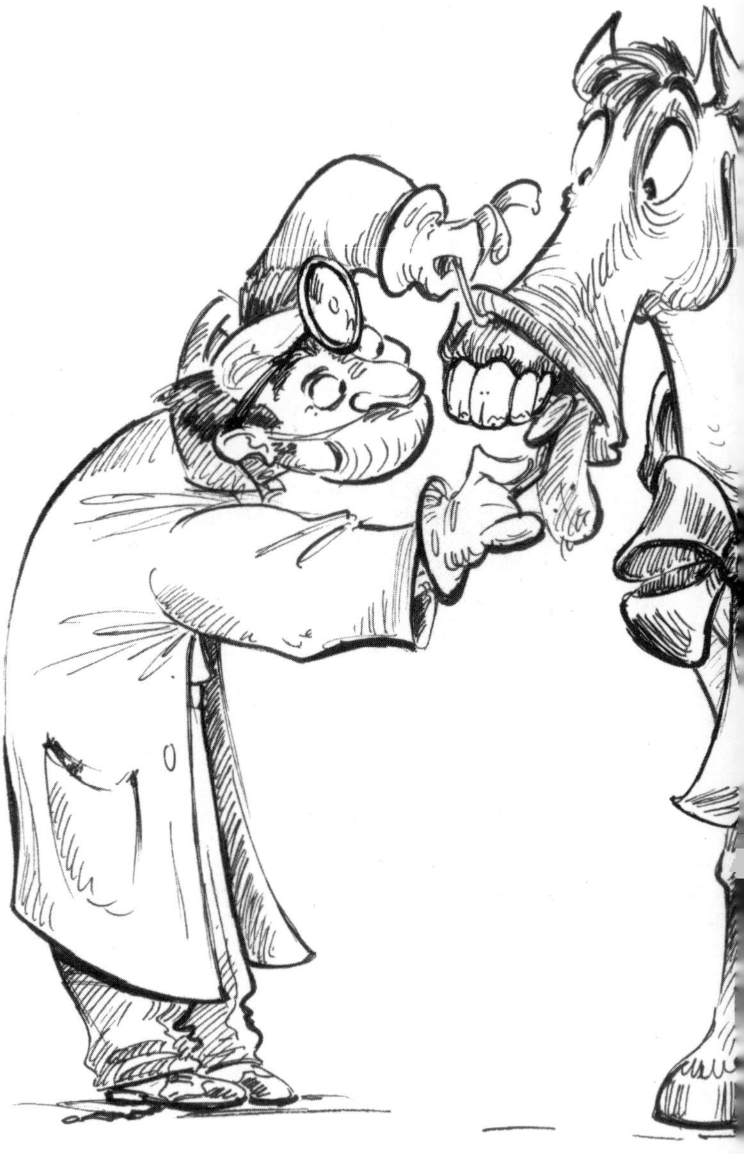

Don't Look a Gift Horse in the Mouth

Estimating a horse's age and health can be done by looking at the condition and number of its teeth. This proverb reminds us to be grateful for the gifts we receive and not look for fault with them. (See also *long in the tooth*.)

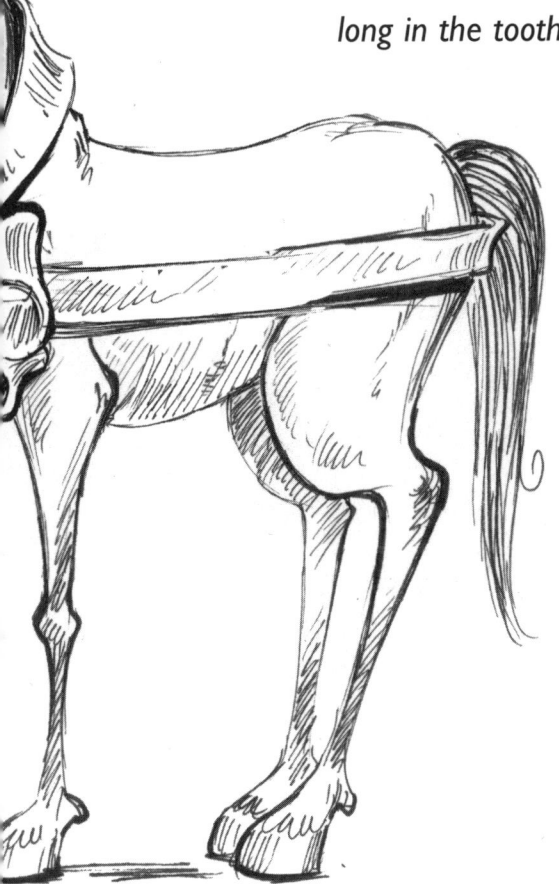

Down to the Wire

A term used to describe a close finish to a horse race. The wire refers to the wire stretching above the racetrack to demarcate the finish line which would help officials determine the winner. The phrase is now used to describe any close finish, and it suggests that an outcome will not be known until the very end. (See also *under the wire*.)

"It came down to the wire whether we would get our proposal in on time."

Fast Track

A dry, hard racing surface that enables horses to run at peak speed. This expression is associated with a situation or position that is a route to rapid or expedited advancement, especially in business or government.

"After only a short time at the firm he was on the fast track to becoming partner."

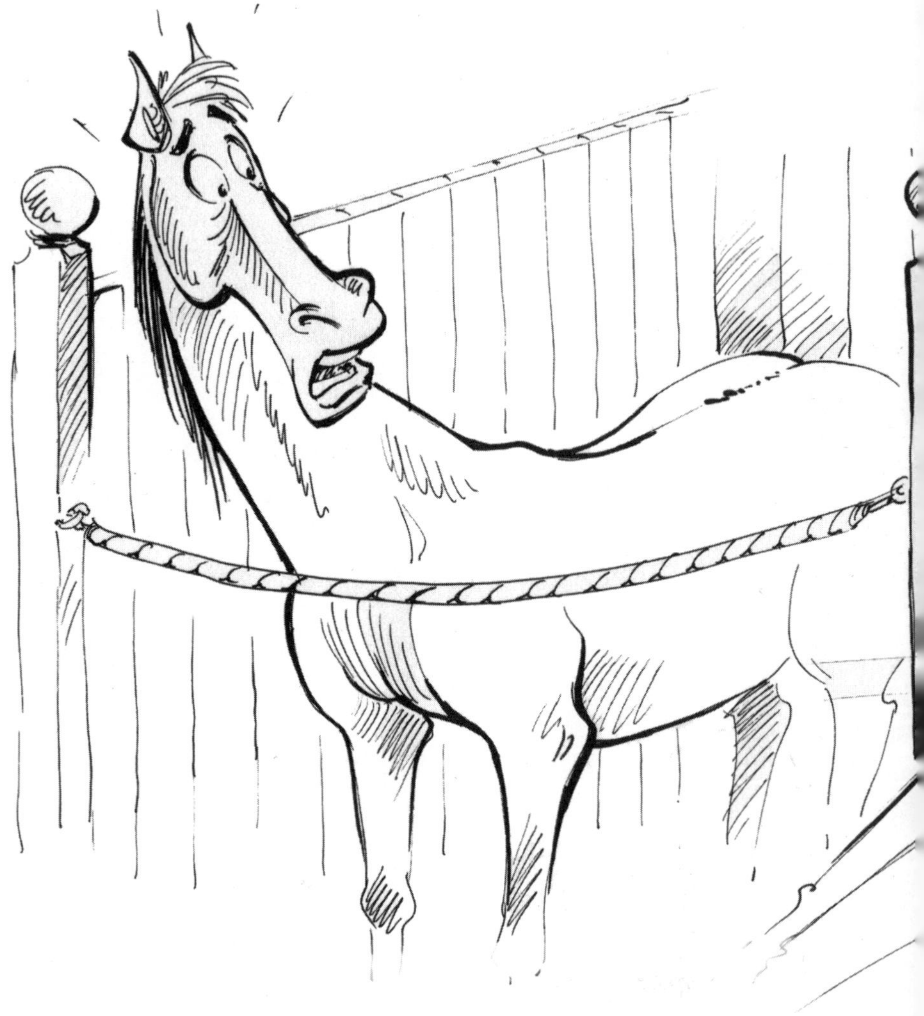

Get Your Goat

Goats have long been used as a calming influence on racehorses. The term refers to a long ago practice of stealing a goat from a horse's stall before a race, making the horse nervous and too unsettled to run a good race. If you walk through a horse barn today you will see many companion animals, however they are rarely stolen. If you are annoyed or bothered, it may be said that someone or something has gotten your goat.

Handicap

A penalty or disadvantage given to a superior horse in an attempt to make the competition more equal. The horses are assigned their additional weight (their "handicap") based upon their past performance. The extra weight carried in the horse's saddle slows it down. In common speech, "handicap" has come to refer to a wide range of disabilities. The word comes from "hand in cap," an old British game of chance in which money was placed in a cap and a neutral umpire set odds.

Handicapper

In horse racing, the handicapper originally referred to the judge who assigns additional weights to the horses in a handicap race. Over time, the meaning of the term has expanded to include anyone with expertise in predicting the winners in a horse race, especially someone who publishes or sells these picks in a newspaper. In common speech, a handicapper is anyone who "handicaps," or tries to determine the chances that any given entrant will win a contest.

"Our political analyst will handicap the primaries leading up to the general election.

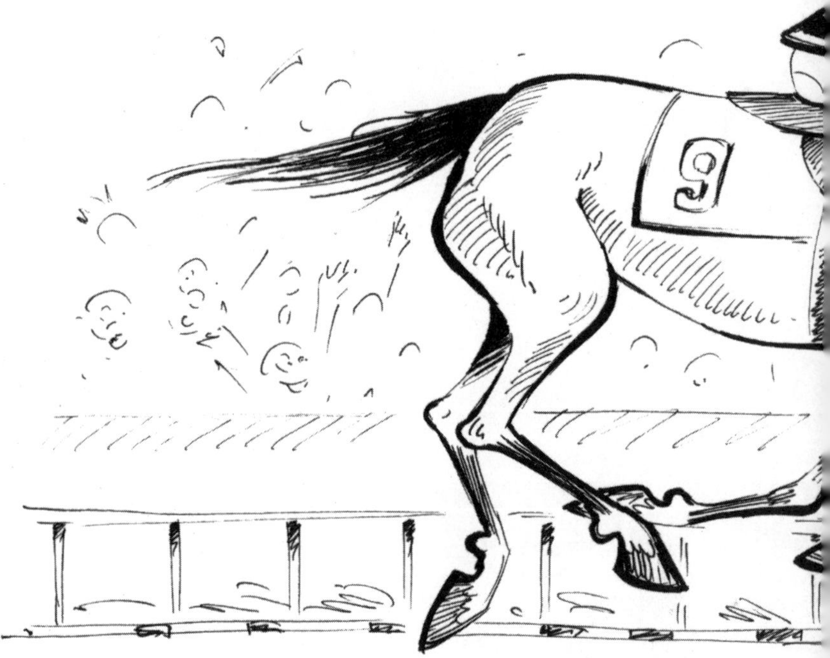
9

Handily or Hands Down

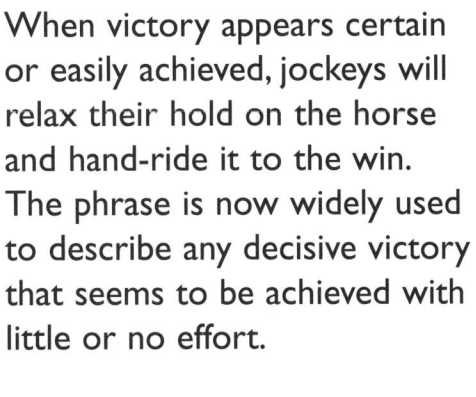

When victory appears certain or easily achieved, jockeys will relax their hold on the horse and hand-ride it to the win. The phrase is now widely used to describe any decisive victory that seems to be achieved with little or no effort.

Here's Mud in Your Eye

A humorous toast, usually among friends. There are many theories on the origin of this phrase, but all connote good spirits and jocularity. Those who attribute the term to horse racing believe it describes the situation in which a horse in the lead kicks dirt or mud into the eyes or face of a horse following behind. Perhaps it signifies a desire for two friends to finish well—the toaster in first, and the toasted a close second.

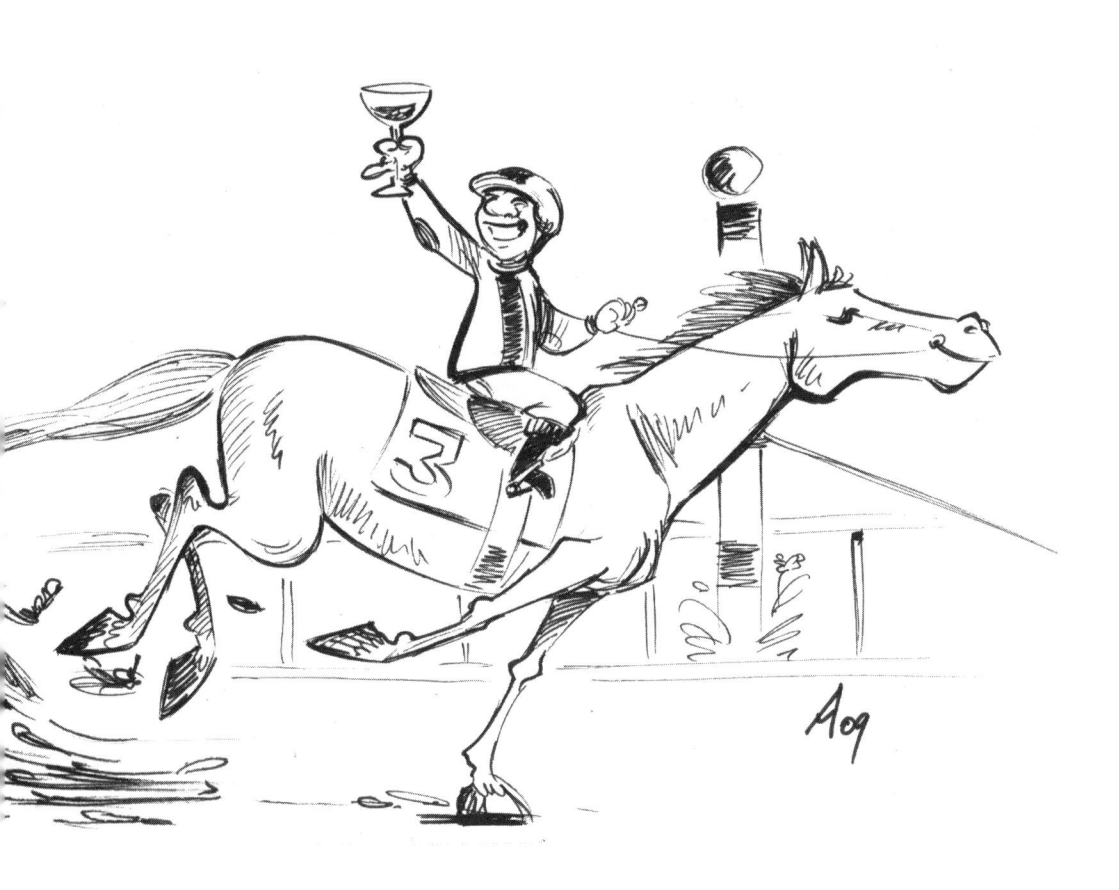
3

Horses for Courses

A handicapping term that indicates a horse has a better record on one track or racing surface than another. The phrase is used outside of horse racing to mean someone who is particularly well suited for a given situation as a result of either being familiar with the environment or having the needed skills to perform well. There are many reasons why a horse may thrive on a certain course, but it often comes down to the horse just liking the surface.

"You've got to pick the right horse for the course. You wouldn't hire a plumber to fix your car!"

Hot to Trot

Most commonly used to describe someone who is enthusiastic and eager to do something. Though not part of racing terminology, it obviously stems from observing racehorses prior to a race. It sometimes takes on a lascivious connotation.

This phrase refers to a horse who is sweating profusely usually just before a race. (It's true—a horse's sweat looks just like soap.) When a horse is in a lather, he is often agitated or anxious and unfocused on the task at hand, which many handicappers consider a bad sign. Now widely used to describe someone who is worked up about a situation or issue.

In a Lather

PLACE WIN SHOW

In the Money

In horse racing, payouts are given for bets made on the horses that win, place, and show. Hence a horse that finishes in the top three has run "in the money." Broadly used to mean having success of any kind or doing well financially. When Ginger Rogers sings "We're in the Money" from the Depression-era musical *Gold Diggers of 1933*, she's thumbing her nose at hard financial times, honoring the riches she has, and celebrating the bright future ahead.

In the Running

Generally used to describe a horse or a person with a place among the leading competitors in a race, it can also be used to describe any contestant entered in a competition. Often applied in the context of a political campaign where multiple candidates have a strong chance of winning the election. Conversely, "out of the running" describes a contestant who has dropped out or no longer has a chance of winning.

Inside Track

In horse racing, where the tracks are oval, the inner side of the track is shorter than the outer. This means that the horse running along the inside rail (the "inside horse") has less ground to cover than the other horses in the field. A person with the inside track holds a competitive advantage or has a more direct route to achieving a goal than his or her rivals. This person may have also have some "inside" knowledge that others do not have.

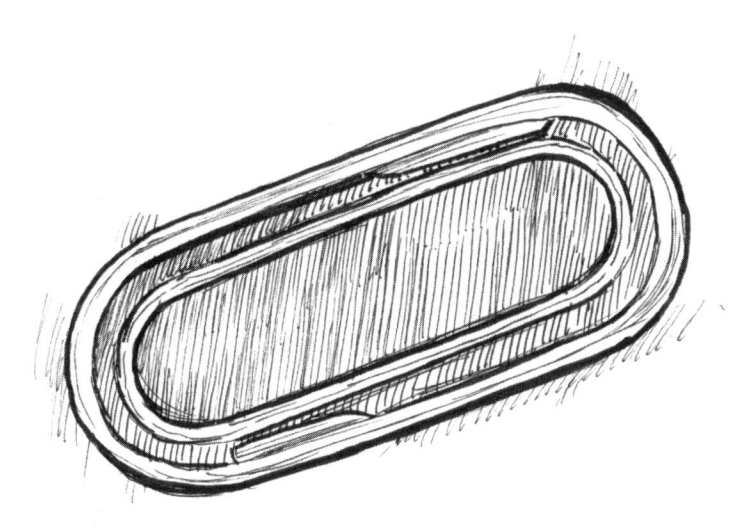

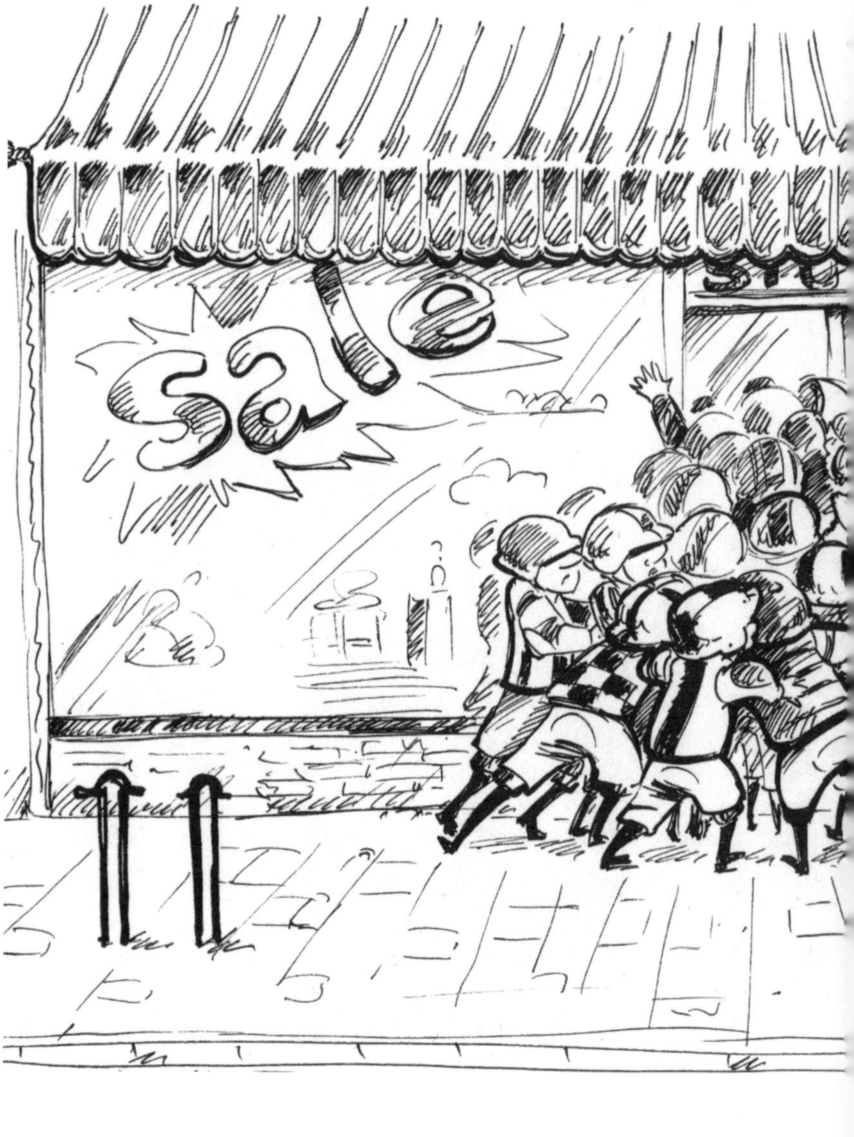
Sale

Jockey for Position

During a race, jockeys steer their horses into the optimal position for winning. For example, a jockey may attempt to get the horse over to the rail to save ground (see *inside track*). The phrase has come to mean any kind of maneuver into position, manipulation, or strategy to gain a competitive edge. It can be used to describe physical jockeying or verbal jockeying, as in a political debate.

The teeth of horses continue to grow as they age. Their gums also recede, making the teeth appear longer and more prominent the older they get. The phrase is commonly used to describe someone who is getting on in years or has a lot of experience. (See also *don't look a gift horse in the mouth*.)

Long in the Tooth

Long Shot

The term originally referred to a shot fired from a distance with one of the early firearms that were rarely accurate. It has been adopted by horse racing as the term for any horse in a race that is unlikely to win but does have a slim chance of doing so. Since favorites often go off at low odds that carry only a small potential payout, some people (like us) find it more enjoyable to bet the long shot. In everyday speech, used to describe anything that is very unlikely to happen.

Neck and Neck

Two or more horses in a race that are keeping even with each other, neither falling behind nor getting ahead, are said to be running "neck and neck." If you're watching a race where this is the case, you're likely to be on your feet and shouting the whole way. These are the kinds of contests that racing fans live for. Often used to describe any tight or close outcome.

Odds-On

The "odds-on" in a race is the horse whose betting line is even money or less. This highly regarded animal is the opposite of the long shot. Refers to anything that is very likely to succeed or happen.

"He's the odds-on to win the Heisman Trophy this year."

Off and Running

When listening to the call of a race the first words you'll commonly hear the announcer say are "They're off and running." This indicates that all horses have left the starting gate and the race is underway. To be off and running is to have started on a course of action and initially to be making good progress.

The phrase does not refer to airplanes or birds or Pegasus but to a race where one or more horses come out of the gate with such a great burst of speed that they get a jump on the field. The person who is off to a flying start has rapidly assumed an advantageous position in any kind of endeavor.

Off to a Flying Start

Off to the Races

At one time, this was a common expression meaning exactly what it says, "I'm off to see the horse races." It is now used to mean an event or competition has begun or that some chain of events has been set in motion. It is often used in association with the launch of something positive or fun.

"When their small business loan was approved, they were off to the races."

On One's High Horse

Commonly used to describe a person who behaves pretentiously or arrogantly. A person on horseback towers over those standing on the ground and has a position of control. The phrase is invoked to deride people who imagine they have an elevated status and use it as an excuse to act superior or lord it over others.

On One's Toes

A horse that is alert and eager. You might not think that a horse would have a toe, but that's what the front part of a horse's hoof or shoe is called. Handicappers often look for horses that are up on their toes in the paddock or when they first step onto the track—it may be a sign that the horses are, to use another racing expression, raring to go. For people the term means being awake and responsive to whatever is coming their way.

> *"The ups and downs of the stock market have really kept investors on their toes."*

On the Money

Originally came from placing a winning wager on a horse in a race. When you were on the money, you picked the right horse to bet on. This phrase has carried over into the mainstream language to mean correct, accurate, or precise. (See also *on the nose*.)

On the Nose

The nose is the smallest possible winning margin in a horse race. To bet on the nose is to bet on the horse that wins. Like "on the money," outside of horse racing this phrase has come to mean getting something just right.

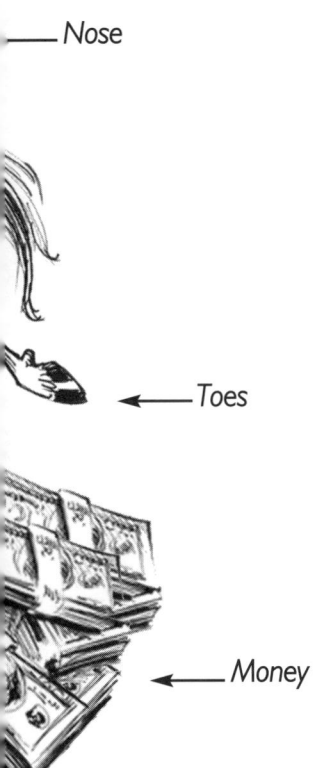

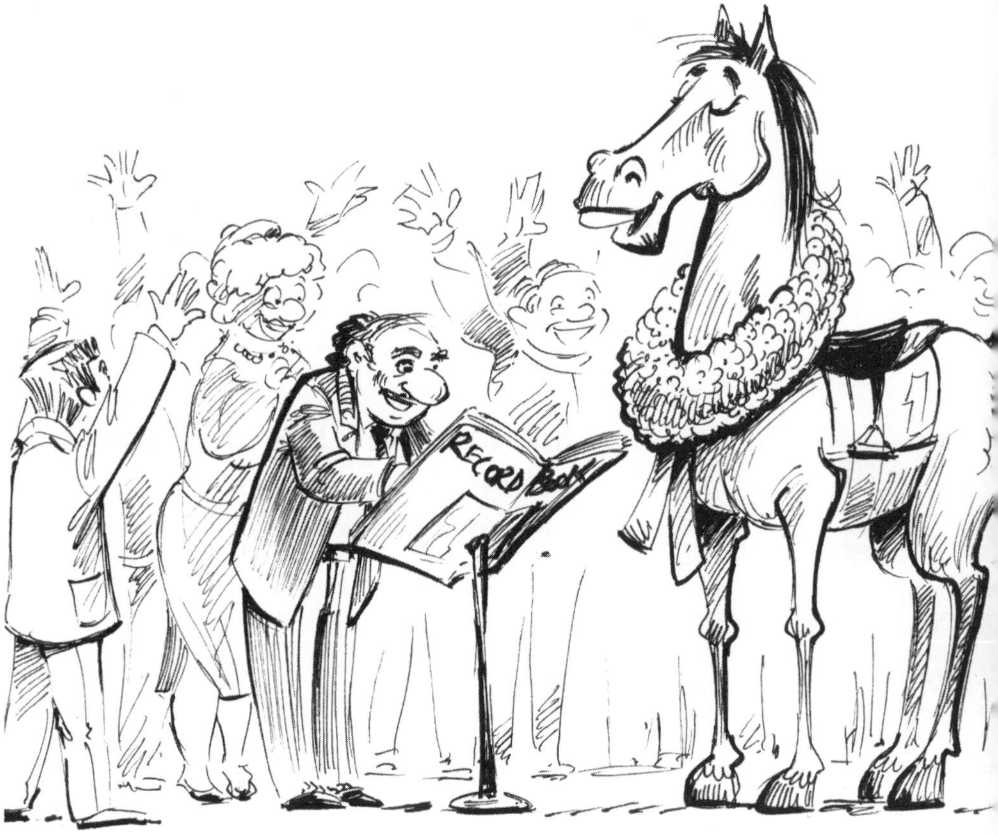
RECORD BOOK

One for the Books

This phrase describes an outstanding or unusual achievement—in sports generally, one that qualifies for the official record books. In horse racing, records of winning times for different courses and distances are compiled. In some circles "one for the books" is thought to have referred originally to a wager that a bookie or bookmaker did not have to pay out on.

Out of the Clouds

The origins of this phrase are misty, but it is commonly used in horse racing journalism to describe a horse that comes from way back to win. Out of the clouds may be similar in meaning to out of a clear blue sky or out of nowhere, but it may also refer to the clouds of dust kicked up by front-runners that the horse from the back of the pack has to race through in order to gain the lead.

"The offer came from out of the clouds and at the last possible moment."

Out of the Gate

Refers to the beginning of a race, just after the horses have departed from a mechanical starting gate. "First out of the gate" describes someone who has started off quickly and has a lead on the competition. (See also *off and running*.)

The end of a race which is so close that the winner is discernable only from a photograph taken as the horses cross the finish line. The first reported use of a camera to document the end of a race was in 1888 at a track in Plainfield, New Jersey. A common variation on "It's a photo finish!" is simply "He wins in a photo!" The term is now widely used to describe any close competition.

Photo Finish

Put Through One's Paces

Originally used in connection with judging a horse's ability to canter, trot, or gallop. It now refers to testing a person's ability or level of skill. Often used in the context of determining someone's capabilities for a job.

"When she applied for her first job, she was put through her paces in a series of tough interviews."

Put Your Money On the Line

Akin to "put your money where your mouth is," this means to demonstrate confidence in your opinions by risking your funds in a wager. The line is thought to refer to the imaginary line between bettor and betting clerk—the place where you lay your money when making a bet. In common speech, this phrase asks that you deliver on what you promise.

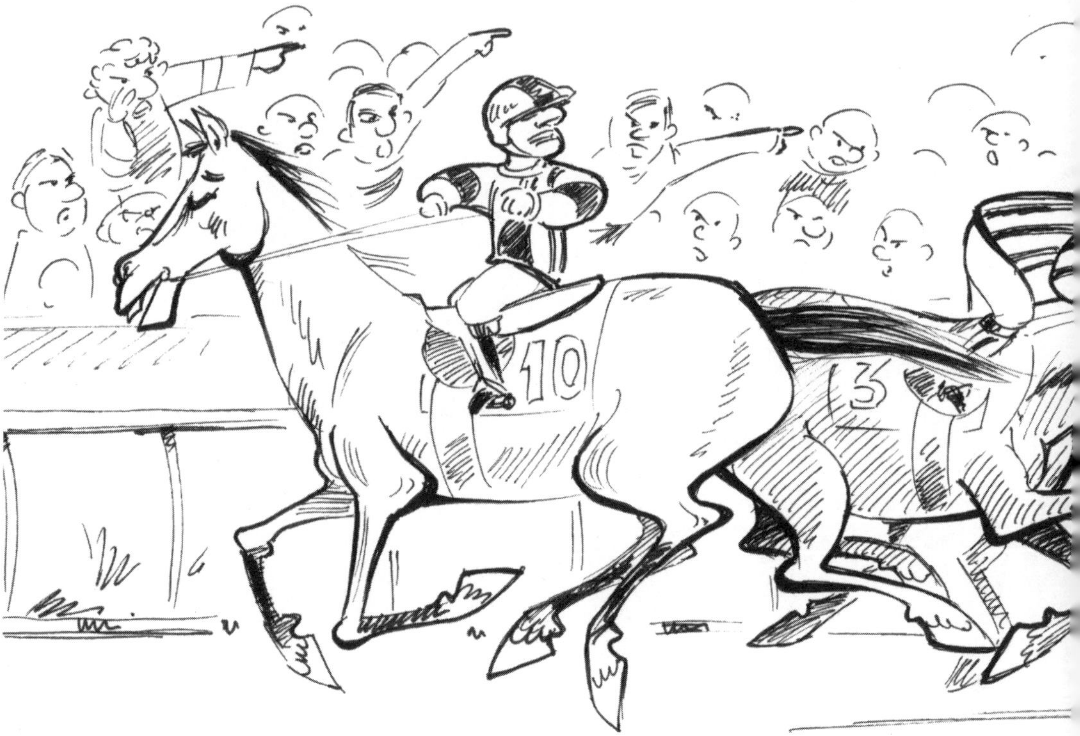
10
3

Rank Outsider

The word *rank* has several meanings, both in the dictionary and when applied to horses. A rank (or complete) outsider is a horse entered at very long odds and not expected to win or have any success at all. A rank (or unruly) horse, on the other hand, is headstrong and difficult to ride. When used to refer to a person, the term seems to combine both meanings: a rank outsider is a person who is viewed as incompetent and ineffectual and considered certain to be a failure.

Ride for a Fall

To ride a horse recklessly or overconfidently, courting disaster. Jockeys who are too aggressive with their horses may create the conditions for a spill that could harm them, their mounts, and other jockeys and horses in a race. The phrase is applied to people who are taking far too big a risk for their circumstances and warns that they will likely get their comeuppance.

Run Circles Around

A horse that runs much better than its rivals, meaning that it laps the field on a circular track. In everyday speech, almost any kind of superiority can be described as being able to "run circles around" the competition. The phrase "run rings around" has the same meaning and origin.

Run True to Form

When handicappers try to assess how well a horse will do in an upcoming race, they often refer to a "form sheet" listing the records of how the horse has done in the past. If the horse then performs in a way that is consistent with its racing history or pedigree, it has "run true to form." Outside the track, the phrase is widely used to refer to any behavior that might have been expected, especially based on prior experience.

"The 6:15 flight ran true to form, departing 20 minutes late."

Set the Pace

In a horse race, a faster horse or horses will establish the tempo—or "set the pace"—for the early part of the race. The other horses adjust their speed depending on their running style. In everyday language, a "pacesetter" is someone who acts as an example for others to equal or rival.

"The company set the pace in the field of biotechnology."

In early organized horse racing, the starting point was a line that someone scratched into the ground. Horses not given a handicap (see entry) would start from the scratched line; horses with a handicap would start ahead of it. The phrase as it is used today means to start from a position of no advantage or knowledge or with nothing but the most basic ingredients. On a related note, in racing a scratched horse is one that has been withdrawn from a race before it begins.

Start from Scratch

A trustworthy tip on a horse in a race. The tip's giver vouches for its accuracy and profitability by stating he's heard it from the highest authority, the horse itself. Used more broadly to indicate information obtained from any authority very close to the subject at hand. The phrase is also related to the examination of a horse's teeth to determine its age or health (see *don't look a gift horse in the mouth*).

Straight from the Horse's Mouth

Take in Stride

To take a hurdle without change of gait, or in stride, was a term that originated with descriptions of horses leaping hedges. It has come to mean being unfazed by an obstacle or something unexpected.

> *"The candidate took his opponent's mudslinging in stride."*

Too Close to Call

Words a track announcer may say at the close of a race in which the winner is not immediately apparent, because two or more horses appear to cross the finish line at the same time (see also *photo finish*). Now widely used to describe electoral races where the winner cannot be predicted because there is too narrow a margin between the candidates.

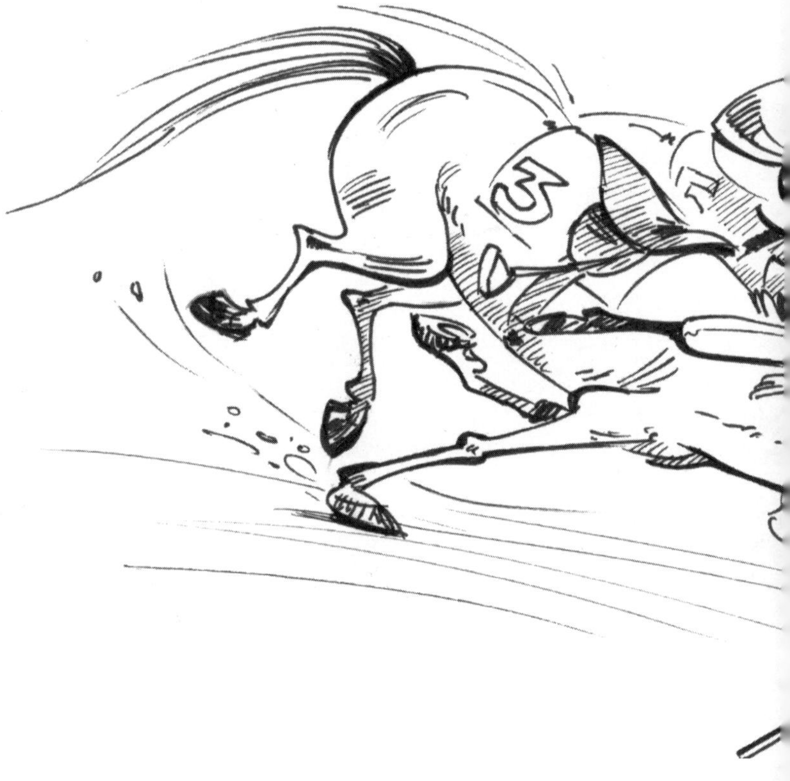

Under the Wire

Refers to the end of a horse race—that moment when horses pass under the wire that marks the finish. Used broadly to mean getting something done at the very last possible moment before it is too late. (See also *down to the wire*.)

Acknowledgments

Working on this book has been an amazingly positive experience for us. It has given us the opportunity to explore what it is we love about horse racing and to share that with others, even with those with limited interest in the sport.

There are a few people we would like to specifically thank for helping us along the way.

First and foremost, we thank our editor, Karen Cook, who read the manuscript with the eye of someone not immersed in the world of horse racing. Her comments, queries, and suggested revisions were invaluable.

Thanks go to our illustrator, Ana Mirela Tache, whose work and collaborative spirit helped bring the pages to life.

We are also grateful to our friend, handicapper Nick Borg, for his humor and encouragement, and for keeping us in the game.

Our great appreciation goes to all our friends and family for their inspiration and support.

And finally, to our very own Cougar cat.

May you all always be "off to the races!"

About the Authors

Bill Tivenan, a former quality assurance analyst for charts and past performances at *The Daily Racing Form*, has been involved with thoroughbred racing for over 20 years. A writer and producer working in film, radio and new media, Bill is a graduate of Berea College and the University of Michigan. He is a member of the Writers Guild of America East (WGAE).

Cassandra Cook is a freelance print and web publishing project manager. A graduate of Vassar College, Cassandra credits her love of language and writing to her parents, Claire and James Cook, both of whom were writers as well as editors. Cassandra thanks her husband, Bill Tivenan, for introducing her to the world of racing and all of the wonderful horses and colorful characters in it.

Ana Mirela Tache, a freelance illustrator and animator is originally from Romania. She now resides in Budapest, Hungary.

To learn more about this book, visit us on the web at
www.offtoaflyingstartpress.com